Snooker

Ken Williams

Produced for A & C Black by

Monkey Puzzle Media Ltd
Gissings Farm, Fressingfield
Suffolk IP21 5SH

Published in 2006 by

A & C Black Publishers Ltd
38 Soho Square, London W1D 3HB
www.acblack.com

Fourth edition 2006

Note: While every effort has been made to ensure
that the content of this book is as technically accurate
and as sound as possible, neither the author nor the
publisher can accept responsibility for any injury or
loss sustained as a result of the use of this material.

A & C Black uses paper produced with elemental
chlorine-free pulp, harvested from managed
sustainable forests.

Acknowledgements
Cover and inside design by James Winrow for
Monkey Puzzle Media Ltd.
The publishers would like to thank Power Glide for
their photographic contribution to this book (pages
10 and 11). Front cover photograph courtesy of Getty
Images. Photographs on pages 4, 5, 6, 8, 17, 18, 19,
20, 21, 27, 31, 35, 37, 43, 46 and 61 courtesy of
Empics. All other photographs by Sylvio Dokov.
Illustrations by Dave Saunders (page 45) and Ron
Dixon at TechType.

KNOW THE GAME is a registered trademark.

Printed and bound in China by C&C Offset Printing Co., Ltd

Note: Throughout this book players and officials are
referred to as 'he'. This should, of course, be taken to
mean 'he or she' where appropriate.

CONTENTS

04 FOREWORD
05 A brief history of snooker

06 EQUIPMENT
06 Table
09 Balls
10 Cue
14 Rests
15 Accessories

16 THE GAME
16 The object balls
16 Placing the balls on the table
17 The object of the game

18 FOULS AND PENALTIES
18 Fouls
19 Penalties

22 THE STANCE
22 Placing the feet and legs
24 Positioning the upper body
26 The movement of the cue arm
27 Summary

28 SIGHTING
28 Methods of sighting

30 THE BRIDGE
30 The bridge hand
31 The bridge arm

32 SHOTS
32 Striking the plain ball
33 Topspin
34 Side
35 Backspin
36 The screw shot
38 The swerve shot
39 The stun

40 POTTING
42 The nap

46 HOW TO PRACTISE
46 Cue-ball control
52 Other important shots

**54 SNOOKER WORLD
   CHAMPIONS 1927–2005**

56 MAXIMUM BREAKS

**58 THE WORLD PROFESSIONAL
   BILLIARDS & SNOOKER
   ASSOCIATION**

59 GLOSSARY

62 INDEX

FOREWORD

This book will provide the beginner with the best possible advice and tuition to make progress in the game. One player in a million has the ability to pot the ball with consummate ease, and for that person the game will appear to be simple. For everyone else it is a good deal more perplexing.

Joe Davis, multiple world champion between 1927 and 1946.

Remember that to become an accomplished player you will have to devote many hours to practice. Understandably, most beginners just want to get on and play games. After all, snooker should primarily be about having fun! However, if you neglect to practise and do nothing but play, your cue-ball control technique will not develop as quickly as it should.

The illustrations in this book cover the following aspects:

- stance
- cueing
- cue-ball control
- sound practice methods.

All the illustrated shots are basic to snooker. Learn them well and you will have a clearer insight into the game.

A BRIEF HISTORY OF SNOOKER

Snooker is played on a billiards table. The exact origins of snooker are not recorded, although it was almost certainly invented in the late 19th century, most probably by British army officers stationed in India. 'Snooker', army slang for a first-year cadet, was used to refer to newcomers to the game and eventually to the game itself.

The game was introduced to England in the 1880s, and annual snooker championships began in 1916. The first world championship took place in 1927 and was won by Joe Davis, the outstanding player of that era. Davis went on to win it 15 times in 20 years.

The television era

After a period of decline in the 1950s and 1960s, snooker received a boost in 1969 when the BBC launched a new tournament, *Pot Black*. The game, and the

characters who played it, caught the public imagination, and *Pot Black* became the second most popular programme on BBC2. The world championships were first televised in 1976 and world rankings were introduced the following year.

Since then, snooker has grown into a game of enduring appeal, regularly attracting big viewing figures. In 2005, the Embassy World Professional Snooker Championship final between Shaun Murphy and Matthew Stevens was watched by a massive late-night audience of nearly 8 million viewers.

▼ Snooker reached a peak of popularity in 1985, when 18.5 million watched Dennis Taylor defeat Steve Davis in the world championship final.

> **Practise the various shots illustrated in this book with a playing partner and you will find it just as entertaining as playing frames – and far more rewarding for your game.**

EQUIPMENT

To play snooker you need a table, balls, cues, rests and
several other accessories – all of which will be available
in your local club. In this section we will look at each of
these items, and offer advice on how to look after them.

TABLE

A full-size snooker table is made
up of a slate bed, 1¹/₂–2 inches
(3.8–5.1cm) thick, incorporated
within a wooden frame. The bed
is covered with a tightly stretched
green woollen cloth called the baize.
The surface of the baize has small
soft fibres, termed the nap, running
from the bottom (baulk) to the top
(black spot) end of the table.

Pockets

There are six pockets, one at each
corner and one exactly in the middle
of each long side. The two at the
black spot end are known as top
pockets and the two at the baulk
end are bottom pockets. The middle
ones are called centre pockets.

Rubber cushions, overhanging by
1¹/₂–2 in (3.8–5.1cm) plus cushion
rails, enclose the playing area. There
is, of course, a gap in the cushion at

A standard snooker table stands 2 ft 9¹/₂ in
to 2 ft 10¹/₂ in (85–87.6cm) from the floor
to the top of the cushion rail.

TABLE DIMENSIONS

The bed of a
standard full-size
snooker table
measures 12 ft x
6 ft (3.66m x 1.87m),
though this can
vary slightly from
manufacturer to
manufacturer.

each place where a pocket is situated, to allow the ball to enter.

Table markings

A line is drawn across the width of the table parallel with the bottom cushion and 29 in (74cm) from its face. This is called the baulk line.

From the centre point of this line, a semi-circle is marked within the baulk area with a radius of 11½ in (29cm). This is called the D. When the player is 'in hand' – that is, when the cue ball is off the table or after it has entered a pocket – the player must take his or her next stroke from the D area. Any point may be chosen, either on the baulk line or within the semi-circular area.

The other markings consist of four spots on an imaginary line travelling lengthwise up the centre of the table. These spots, marked with very small wafer-like pieces of silk or by tailor's chalk, are positioned as follows:

- at the centre of the baulk line, known as the brown spot
- at the centre of the table itself, known as the centre spot (or blue spot)
- halfway between the centre spot and the face of the top cushion, known as the pyramid spot (or pink spot)
- 12¾ in (32.4cm) from the face of the top cushion, known as the spot (or black spot)
- the two other spots used – the yellow spot and the green spot – are located at the corners of the D.

The snooker table

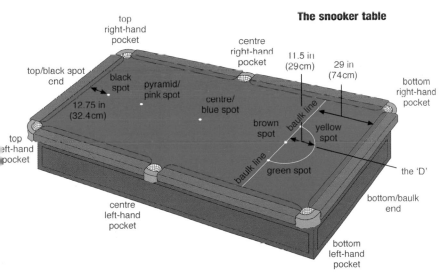

top right-hand pocket

centre right-hand pocket

11.5 in (29cm)

29 in (74cm)

top/black spot end

black spot

pyramid/ pink spot

centre/ blue spot

brown spot

baulk line

yellow spot

bottom right-hand pocket

12.75 in (32.4cm)

top left-hand pocket

baulk line

green spot

the 'D'

centre left-hand pocket

bottom/baulk end

bottom left-hand pocket

7

Care of the table

1. The table should be brushed with a special table brush either before or after each day's play. Brush firmly but not vigorously since there is little point in sending dust or dirt into the air only for it to settle on the table again.

   Always brush from the baulk end towards the black spot end – that is, with the nap. Brush in straight lines so that dust and dirt are neatly gathered under the top cushion. Then, with the shaped end of the brush, sweep the accumulated dust gently into one of the pockets, shaking the latter immediately to make sure that the dust does not settle there.

2. When brushing has been completed, it is a good idea to draw a baize-covered pad up the table in long, continuous, straight strokes.

3. Ironing should be done with a special iron that should be tested for heat before applying it to the cloth. When you judge the iron to be ready, place it briefly on a piece of newspaper. If the paper discolours even slightly the iron is too hot. Once satisfied that there is no risk of burning the cloth, draw the iron up the table in a baulk-to-spot direction. Use long, continuous, straight strokes, holding it at a slight angle to the cushions and without

The referee carefully places the pink ball on its slot. Care should always be taken with the surface of the table.

coming into contact with them. Remember, cushions are made of rubber!

PLACING BALLS

When placing any ball on its spot, always place it to one side of the spot and slide it gently into place without applying any pressure, as this could make a friction burn – a flat spot on the ball surface. Banging a ball down on a spot merely risks creating a hole in the cloth.

BALLS

When playing on a full-size table, snooker balls must be $2^1/_{16}$ in (5.25cm) in diameter. Smaller sizes are available for small tables.

Care of the balls

Avoid keeping balls in extremely hot or extremely cold conditions. Keeping the balls clean is absolutely crucial. Before playing, it is a good idea to wipe the balls with a damp cloth and polish them dry with a dry cloth. Failing this, always make sure that the cue ball is clean before the start of each frame. The longer that balls are used without cleaning, the more likely it is that spots of dirt and chalk will become ingrained and affect their performance.

Make sure you don't mix one set of balls with another. If the cue ball is either heavier or lighter than the other balls it will affect the angles at which it rebounds from them.

CUE

The snooker cue is a sophisticated piece of equipment and the most important part of your armoury. Before you buy a cue of your own you will have to make do with a cue from the communal rack at the club where you play. The best cues allow you to perform all the functions demanded of them.

Parts of the cue

A cue is a tapered wooden stick with a circular cross-section. The end with the larger circumference is the butt, and the narrow end is the tip. A ferrule attached to the tip holds the leather cue tip (this reduces wear on the cue from replacing tips over the years). The large, lower section of the cue is called the cue butt, and the thinner section is the shaft.

Cue length

Most cues are produced to a standard length of 4 ft 10 in (147cm). However, bear in mind that a length of approximately 4 ft 8$\frac{1}{2}$ in (143cm) does produce a more powerful cue.

Materials

The most popular material for the shaft of the cue is straight-grained ash. The grain should not be too wide: about ten grain lines to the inch (four to the centimetre) looks good and is sufficient to supply the required shaft strength. Maple is also a perfectly good material, but because of its density it does tend to push the cue ball off the intended line when 'side' is applied (see page 34).

When choosing a snooker cue, remember to consider the quality of the wood, the weight and the balance.

Weight and balance

The most popular weight for a cue is between 17 oz (482g) and 17$\frac{1}{2}$ oz (496g), with the weight balancing forwards when the cue is suspended on the finger at the top of the butt splicing. The forward weight in the shaft is the key to a well-balanced and correctly powered cue. A cue that is overweighted to the back tends to rise off the bridge during the execution of the stroke.

Cue tips

Cue tips are made of elk leather of varying degrees of hardness. There are different diameters of cue tip, but generally speaking a diameter of 0.38 in (9.75 mm) allows the ball to hold its intended line more accurately. However, you should bear in mind that the tip size could vary depending on the stress strength of any particular piece of timber used in the cue.

TYPES OF CUE

Cues come in one- and two-piece models. The cheaper cues, often found in the communal rack, tend to be one-piece. Two-piece cues have metal joints that can be unscrewed for ease of transport.

Fitting and shaping a new cue tip

Fitting and shaping your tip is easy, with the right equipment.

1. First clean and level the brass ferrule and wood with a cue ferrule leveller.

2. Rub the base of the cue tip on a piece of fine sandpaper to remove any indentations or manufacturer's tip dressing. Make sure the base of the tip is perfectly flat and level.

3. Apply a top-quality instant tip adhesive, and position the tip. Apply pressure with the thumb for about 10 seconds. Set aside for a few minutes before trimming and shaping. If an oversize tip is used, turn the cue onto its tip and trim with a sharp blade.

Chalk

It is impossible to overstate the importance of using a good-quality billiard chalk. It must be of the correct grit and make-up – too hard and the chalk will not adhere to the cue tip; too soft and powdery and it will stick to the ball and foul the cloth. The latter is one of the major reasons for what are commonly referred to as 'kicks' – irregular movements of the cue ball.

Equally, the cue tip must be made up of a fibre that can receive the chalk. If the tip is too hard the chalk

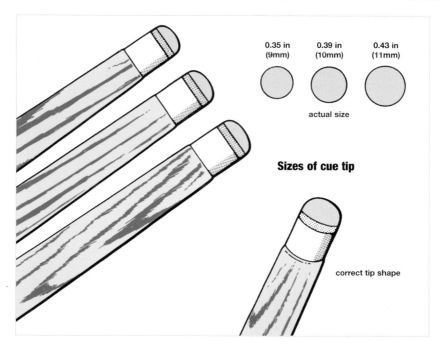

0.35 in (9mm) 0.39 in (10mm) 0.43 in (11mm)

actual size

Sizes of cue tip

correct tip shape

will not adhere; if it is too soft the fibres will break up, preventing a proper feel between cue tip and ball.

Chalking the cue tip

The act of chalking the cue tip is not treated with a great deal of reverence by the large majority of snooker players. All players are aware that chalk helps to eliminate miscues, but not all understand the importance of correctly applying it to the tip. The chalk should be held in either hand in a stationary position at a slight angle. When the cue is rotated, this action tends to shape the top half of the tip correctly. The chalk should never be scrubbed

onto the tip. Used correctly, the chalk will form a tidy hole in its top.

LOOKING AFTER THE CHALK BLOCK

It is a good idea to rub the face of the chalk block on a piece of sandpaper from time to time. This takes the side of the chalk down at the same pace as the hole, avoiding the disastrous rubbing of the chalk edges below the brass ferrule.

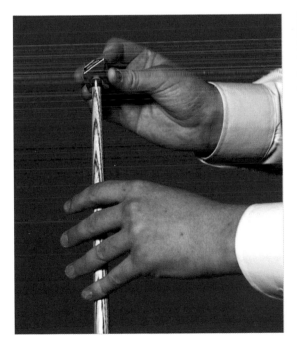

Chalk is applied to the tip in order to increase the friction when the cue hits the cue ball, and to reduce the risk of a miscue.

RESTS

Various designs of cue rests are available to assist you at those times when it is not possible to reach the cue ball with your normal stance.

The standard rest is a stick with a metal or plastic cross at the end, forming a bridge. Different lengths are available: the short, or half-butt, rest is 8 ft (2.4m) long, while the long rest is 12 ft (3.6m) long. A long cue is provided for each of these rests.

There are also positions in which the player cannot easily contact the cue ball because another ball is close to it. A variety of rests have been developed to deal with this difficulty. The hook rest is similar to the standard rest except for its hooked metal end, which allows it to be set around another ball. The spider rest provides a bridge of extra height. The swan has a single extended neck with a fork-like prong at the end to give extra distance over large obstructions.

Many modern players make frequent use of a custom-made extension to reach a remote cue ball. This allows the player to lengthen his or her own cue as necessary, making life more comfortable.

From the top: the extended spider, the swan, the spider and the standard rest.

ACCESSORIES

There are several other items that will be useful to you as a regular snooker player, and it is very important to choose these with care.

A cue case to accompany your cue is more important than some other accessories on the market. Cue cases are available in one- and two-piece models. Quality can vary dramatically, depending on the price.

Another very important purchase is your cue tip (see page 11). Always choose the best-quality tip available. Select the tip that has the right kind of texture and hardness – not too hard, not too soft. A Blue Elk-style tip is by far the most popular choice among top players.

A variety of other utility items are available, such as chalk cubes, cue tip adhesives, cue tip shapers, ferrule levellers, cue cleaners and silicon polishes. Generally speaking, choose the best-quality accessories you can afford, as they can end up making a significant difference to the quality of your game.

THE TRIANGLE OR RACK

The triangle, or rack is the triangular wooden frame used for gathering the red balls into the formation required at the start of each new frame.

There are many companies selling snooker accessories to the enthusiast. Buy the best you can afford.

A selection of cue cases: rigid ones protect your cue best.

THE GAME

Snooker may be played by two or more players, either independently or as teams. The game uses 22 balls: the cue ball (white) and 21 object balls. Each player uses the cue ball in turn to strike one of the object balls.

THE OBJECT BALLS

The object balls, with their values, are as follows:

- 15 red balls (1 point each)
- the yellow ball (2 points)
- the green ball (3 points)
- the brown ball (4 points)
- the blue ball (5 points)
- the pink ball (6 points)
- the black ball (7 points).

The yellow, green, brown, blue, pink and black balls are known collectively as 'the colours'. Any of the colours may be potted after the potting of a red ball. When all of the reds have been potted, the colours must be potted in the ascending order of their value – that is, yellow first, then green, and so on up to black.

PLACING THE BALLS ON THE TABLE

The balls are placed in the positions shown in the illustration below. The 15 red balls form a pyramid or triangular pack – hence the expression 'to break the pack', which means to disturb the opening formation of red balls. The triangle is used to set up the reds in this way. The apex red should be as near as possible to the pink ball without touching it. The six colours are placed on their respective spots, as shown.

The position of the balls

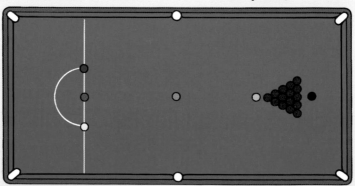

THE OBJECT OF THE GAME

The game's object is to pot as many balls as possible, in the correct order, to win frames and ultimately the game. A red ball is potted first, then any colour, then another red, then a colour, and so on until all 15 reds are pocketed. The reds remain in the pocket each time they are potted, but each time a colour is potted it is retrieved from the pocket and replaced on its own spot.

After all the red balls have been cleared from the table, the six colours remain. These must be potted in the aforementioned order.

Mark Williams on his way to a maximum 147 break in the 2005 world championships.

After the black ball is potted, the game is finished. The winner is the player who gains the higher number of points.

The game described above is a 'frame' of snooker, and a match consists of a given number of frames, which may be anything from a single frame up to any number so long as it is odd (as this allows for a winner).

When a player makes a number of pots in succession, it is called a break.

FOULS AND PENALTIES

A stroke is played when a player strikes the cue ball with the tip of the cue. There are several rules that must be borne in mind when playing a stroke.

When playing a stroke, at least one foot must always be in contact with the ground. If the cue ball is too far away, use a rest.

FOULS

A player must not:

- push the cue ball with the cue, instead of striking it
- force a ball (or balls) off the table
- play a stroke with both feet off the ground
- play a stroke before the balls have come to rest
- touch the ball other than with the cue tip, for example with his or her hand or clothing
- touch the ball with the cue tip before delivering a stroke

- use the 'jump shot', by which the cue ball is made to leap over another ball by hitting it very low down
- use a dead ball to test whether a ball will pass another, or go on a spot, or for any other purpose
- direct the cue ball into a pocket ('to go in-off'), whether it strikes another ball or balls or not
- pot a ball out of the correct order – for example, by potting one red then another red, instead of a colour

- fail to hit the ball the player has nominated after a foul by the player's opponent
- move a ball that is touching the cue ball, instead of playing away from it without moving it
- strike two balls simultaneously unless both are red balls, or one is the ball nominated and the other is the ball on
- snooker (see page 21) with the ball nominated after a foul, unless only pink and black balls remain on the table
- commit a foul after potting a red ball before nominating or attempting to play a colour. The penalty is seven points.

PENALTIES

The penalties for the various fouls are given in the official rule book, obtainable from the World Professional Billiards & Snooker Association, 27 Oakfield Road, Clifton, Bristol BS8 2AT.

AFTER A FOUL STROKE

After a foul stroke by the opponent, a player may play from the current position or ask the opponent to play the next stroke. If the opponent fails again, he or she can again be asked to play the next stroke.

As a general principle, the penalties for most fouls are calculated according to the values of the balls involved in the foul, and the player forfeits the value of the highest. As the minimum penalty is four points, it follows that the forfeit value of the red, yellow and green balls will be four in each case – not one, two and three respectively.

Careful cue control ensures that Ronnie O'Sullivan avoids making a foul shot.

Here are some examples of fouls where the value of the higher ball determines the penalty:

- a player on red strikes black – seven points forfeit (or, as is commonly said, 'seven away')

- a player on black strikes red – seven points forfeit. Both here and in the above example the black value – seven – is the higher and therefore determines the forfeit

- a player on red strikes blue – five away. The blue value – five – is higher than the red forfeit value – four

- black is the ball on, but after the player has hit it, it cannons onto the blue and pots it. The penalty is seven points, the highest value involved.

Penalties for multiple fouls

There is also a rule stating that the first impact governs all strokes, but this does not always apply if two or more fouls are involved in the stroke. Here are some examples:

- a player on blue strikes green. The cue ball, still moving, contacts pink, which enters a pocket, and the player then fouls black with the cue. In this case the forfeit is seven

- a player pots yellow, and then fouls pink with the cue after the cue ball has stopped. The penalty is six points and the yellow is re-spotted

- a player snookers (see page 21) with the nominated ball (free ball). The penalty is the value of the ball on. Therefore, if the player chooses black as the

The referee keeps a close eye on Stephen Hendry. If his arm touches the green ball, it will be a foul.

nominated ball after a foul, when the green is on, and then snookers with the black, the penalty is only four points

- a player is on a red and hits it, but the cue ball goes on to strike black and then goes into a pocket. The penalty is four points – the first impact (which governs all strokes) was on the red, for which the penalty is the minimum: four

- a player on red is snookered after a foul. The player nominates black, fails to hit it, and strikes a red, also potting

black. The penalty is four points because black – the nominated ball – acquires the value of the red for which it was nominated, and therefore also acquires its penalty value.

SNOOKERING

Snookering your opponent increases the chance of them committing a foul. You do this by leaving the cue ball behind a ball that is not 'on', thus blocking its path to a ball that is on. For example, if the next ball on is a red, you can snooker your opponent by positioning the cue ball behind a colour.

In competition play it is the referee's job to be on the lookout for fouls, though it is good etiquette to own up if you commit one.

THE STANCE

The stance you choose when preparing to play a shot is absolutely crucial to your performance. The position of your legs and your arms can be the difference between making and missing a pot.

In this section we will look at recommended positions for feet and legs and the ideal cue action. This is a separate topic from the sighting of the cue ball (see A, page 28). Please note that all references to stance in this section assume that the player is right-handed. If you are left-handed simply swap 'right leg' for 'left leg', and so on.

PLACING THE FEET AND LEGS

Take a look at the photograph of position 1 below. There is no single, ideal position for the feet relative to the cue-arm position shown here. The right foot can be placed in various positions: dead in line, or inside or outside the vertical cue arm.

Position 1

The right foot

The position of the right foot is critical because it affects the follow-through line of the cue after contact with the cue ball. After the follow-through, if the cue finishes to the left of the follow-through line, the shot will almost certainly be missed to the right of the target pocket. Conversely, if the cue finishes to the right of the follow-through line the shot may be missed to the left of the target pocket. With these facts clear in your mind, experiment with various foot positions until the correct follow-through line is mastered. Study 'the straight pot' on page 40 for a visual explanation of the cause and effect of cue deviation from the straight line.

The right leg

Your right leg should be approximately five degrees back from vertical, but not stretched. The photograph of position 1 illustrates this. The photograph of position 2 shows the right leg forwards of vertical. This is incorrect. Note that if the leg is kept in the vertical position, it tends to stop the body getting into a correct, flat-plane position – hence the importance of the back leg angle.

The left leg

Having decided on the most effective position for your right leg and foot, the left leg should be placed in a firm, comfortable position with the leg bent and slightly forward, as shown in the photograph of position 1.

Position 2

Correct (position 1) and incorrect (position 2) leg positions.

Do not attempt to correct your follow-through in mid-action. Your action should be one motion – perfectly smooth and relaxed.

The angle of the feet

This is a somewhat contentious issue. Some professionals keep their feet parallel to the cue line, while others set the feet off at a small angle. It is certainly the case that setting the feet parallel to the cue line can have the effect of straightening the cue's follow-through. The decision is yours. Experiment until you find what works best for you.

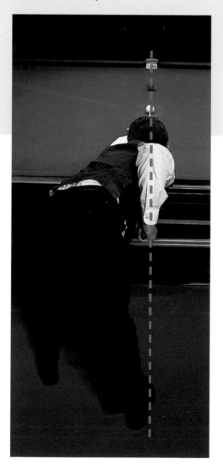

POSITIONING THE UPPER BODY

In a correct stance, the head, right arm and cue all need to be lined up in the direction of the shot. This is well illustrated in the photograph below. We will look at each element of this stance in turn.

Getting into position

First point the cue towards the shot, extending your left arm and bridging hand in the same direction. As you go forward and down into position, extend your left arm while gently pulling your right arm back. This helps to line up the head, turns the shoulders and brings the cue in against the body. The left arm

Note how the right foot, right elbow and head are all aligned in the direction of the shot.

Most players gently touch the cue with the chin for most shots. This helps to reduce your eyes' three-dimensional view to a more two-dimensional image, making long-distance aiming easier.

should rest on the table, slightly bent. Your right hand should grip the cue in a soft but firm manner. The wrist should not be floppy.

The right upper arm

The right upper arm is a crucial element in the correct stance. If it is not aligned, the forearm will not be able to deliver a smooth, straight stroke, the head will want to move, and the feet may be destabilised. To align the upper arm it helps to place your right foot and bridging hand in a reasonably straight line behind the shot.

The elbow

The right elbow should remain in a fixed position when playing a shot, so that the lower right arm pivots consistently from this point. Think of your elbow and lower arm as a pendulum. The swing of this pendulum needs to be only as long as is necessary to produce the power required for any shot. For example, a long stun shot will require a longer swing than a short stun shot (see page 39).

It is vital that all these aspects of stance come together in order to be able to play consistently to a high standard.

See how the right elbow acts as a fixed pivot from which the lower right arm can swing freely yet consistently.

THE MOVEMENT OF THE CUE ARM

It does not matter how accurately you visually judge the shot you are about to play – if you do not deliver the cue tip to its intended target on the cue ball with the right amount of strength, the shot will be missed. Therefore, the movement of the cue arm is of fundamental importance.

The swing

The cue arm should always be vertical, as shown in the photograph below. It should pivot from a fixed point at the elbow with a controlled swing length roughly equal backwards and forwards of the fixed point. The length of the swing should be determined by the power required to play the particular shot.

Over-swinging, which may be intended to produce more power, should be avoided if at all possible since the elbow pivot point will almost certainly be unlocked, and the cue arm thrown off its true line. Unless a player happens to possess a naturally straight action, using too much power almost inevitably results in an inaccurate delivery of the cue.

Notice how the cue arm is vertical. The cue is being held lightly but firmly.

Cueing discipline is all-important. You should try to use the same stance and cueing action with every shot you play.

Don't forget: when striking the cue ball, the eyes should be focused on the object ball.

Keeping still

Perhaps the most important thing to remember is to keep your head and body as still as possible during the shot. The slightest of movements can disturb your aim. Only the right forearm and cue should move. If your head moves it will affect the movement of the cue tip, causing you to miss the predetermined contact points on the cue ball and object ball, inevitably resulting in a poor positional shot or missed pot.

Remember – the most crucial as well as the most difficult task in snooker is to hit the predetermined contact point on the cue ball.

Your eyes can move up and down the line between cue, cue ball and object ball while you are lining up the shot, but at the moment the shot is played it is essential to be looking at the line passing through the object ball.

SUMMARY

If you aspire to be a good snooker player, the disciplines covered in this section are absolutely essential. The three key elements to remember are:

- the position of the head and feet (see photograph on page 22)

- the alignment of right foot with right elbow (see photograph on page 24)

- and the movement of the cue arm (see photograph on page 26).

SIGHTING

Some very fortunate players seem to be able to pot the ball effortlessly – they have the gift of a correct stance and sighting. Here, we look at sighting, a skill most of us have to work at developing.

METHODS OF SIGHTING

There are three methods of sighting, as shown in photographs A, B and C. The correct method for you depends on whether you are left-eyed, right-eyed or even-sighted.

• Photograph A shows the two-eyed sighting style, which is the best method for even-sighted people. Here, the cue is placed centrally under the chin.

Photograph A shows the two-eyed sighting style, arguably the best method for even-sighted people.

Photograph B illustrates a left-eyed sighting, used when the left eye is dominant.

- Photograph B illustrates a left-eyed sighting. The left eye is dominant and the right eye plays very little part. The cue is placed under the left side of the chin so that the left eye is over the ball.

- Photograph C shows a right-eyed sighting, used when the right eye is dominant. The cue is placed under the right side of the chin so that the right eye is over the ball.

The eye–cue relationship

You also must bear in mind the relationship between the eye and the cue. The eye doing the sighting should be directly over the cue. It is very easy, while lining up a shot, for the cue to move out of line with the eye and settle somewhere between the eye and the bridge of the nose. This will impair your ability to sight the centre of the cue ball accurately. What you see as the centre of the cue ball is not in fact the centre, causing you to hit across the ball and apply unintended side.

CHANGING YOUR STYLE

To most players it doesn't matter which is their dominant eye, they naturally play to their style. However, if you are consistently missing shots in the same manner this may be due to your sighting style. If this is the case then you *may* be able to improve your game by experimenting with the other sighting styles.

Photograph C shows a right-eyed sighting, used when the right eye is dominant.

THE BRIDGE

The form of the bridge hand and its grip on the cloth are as important as any other facet of cueing action.

THE BRIDGE HAND

Ideally, the bridge should be formed with the knuckles of the hand raised into a fairly high position, with the fingers firmly out and spread wide, enabling you to grip the cloth firmly. However, bridge hands vary dramatically and, in truth, it is not that important what shape your bridge hand takes so long as it is firm and strong. A soft, floppy bridge hand will definitely be a handicap to your game.

Try also to keep your bridge hand as rigid as possible. Make sure your fingers grip the cloth firmly. If possible, keep your bridge hand at a reasonably constant distance from the cue ball. As a general guide, the distance from the point where the cue rests over the bridge to the cue ball should be about 12 inches (30cm).

> If you find that your bridge hand is floppy, practise flexing the bridge and fingers on a firm surface when not actually playing.

The orthodox bridge, with the palm of the hand slightly raised from the playing surface.

This bridge hand is too floppy.

Bridging on the cushion.

Here the bridge has been elevated to enable the player to hit a shot over an obstructing ball.

Awkward bridging

Do not let awkward bridging throw you. Various hand positions can be adopted for getting over the tops of balls, for bridging off the cushion, and for screwing the ball with the dropped bridge thumb. The photographs on the opposite page show examples of these. Be versatile. Develop your own techniques.

THE BRIDGE ARM

There are many bridge arm positions, and it would be understandable if the beginner was a little confused as to which one to use. One commonly preferred style is to thrust the arm as straight as possible from the shoulder, while keeping it relaxed and comfortable. Taller players often find it easier to bend the arm slightly, so that the sighting of the cue ball is not impaired. Observe the various positions adopted by the professionals, and try one that feels comfortable. If it works, stick with it.

> **REST TECHNIQUE**
>
> When using a rest, use the angle that suits you. Find a distance between the rest head and the cue ball that allows a smooth, flowing action. Too close and the cue will be angled, accentuating any unintentional side. Too far and it will be difficult to play a smooth shot. When playing the shot, don't get down too low; lift your chin sufficiently to allow the butt to pass underneath it.

Most modern players, such as John Higgins here, keep the bridge arm slightly bent. This contrasts with Joe Davis and many from his era, who adopted a straight bridge arm.

SHOTS

The cue ball can be struck in different ways in order to affect the way it moves and the way it influences the movement of the object ball. Hitting the cue ball anywhere apart from dead centre will impart varying degrees of push, affecting its speed, direction and the angle it bounces off the cushion.

STRIKING THE PLAIN BALL

The plain ball is the central point on the surface of the cue ball – that is, the point directly facing the cue. If the cue ball is struck on the plain ball, it will travel in an absolutely straight line towards the object ball. This is the first kind of shot you should master, and it should be at the heart of your playing technique. In fact, if you were able to attain perfect position on every shot played, you would probably never have to use any other kind of shot.

Almost all missed shots are caused by not striking the plain ball, thereby applying unintended side. Accurate plain-ball striking depends, first and foremost, on a good cue action (see pages 22–31). The long straight pot (see page 40) is one of the best tests of your ability to strike the plain ball.

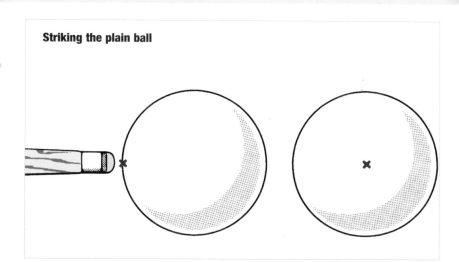

Striking the plain ball

TOPSPIN

The application of topspin (or 'top') creates a dramatic looking snooker shot with the cue ball surging forward and appearing to pick up speed once it has made contact with the object ball. However, as with all shots, it will only be useful in certain situations.

Topspin is generated every time your cue hits the cue ball above the plain ball, i.e. dead centre. The higher up you strike it, the more top is applied. It is not as easy as it may appear. It is very easy to apply unintended side by hitting the ball top right or top left instead of top centre. It is also very important to strike the cue ball on a level plane. Therefore you must raise your bridge hand to the height of the required contact point.

SIGHTING THE BALL ACCURATELY

Plain-ball striking is the only way you can tell if you are sighting the cue ball accurately.

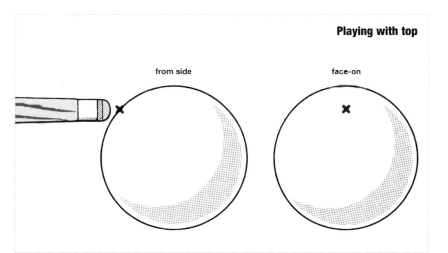

Playing with top

from side   face-on

SIDE

Playing with 'side' means applying side spin to the ball. This is done by striking the ball to the left or right of centre, affecting how the cue ball travels towards the object ball. A ball struck to the right of centre will move to the left, and a ball struck to the left of centre will move to the right.

This sounds simple enough, but it is actually one of the most complex and difficult shots in snooker, causing more problems for the novice than almost any other aspect of cue-ball control. Things to bear in mind when playing side include:

- how much side spin is being applied? The closer to the extreme edge of the ball, the more it will spin and the more its direction will be affected

- what is the distance between the cue ball and the object ball? When the effects of the spin cease, the cue ball will start to come back to its original line. The ideal distance is 12–18 in (30–45cm) from the object ball. Any further away and the cue ball will come back to the side to which the side was applied

- how hard is the shot being played? It is essential that the shot is played with sufficient forward momentum to ensure that the cue ball deviates to the smallest extent possible from the straight path of cue ball to object ball.

Playing with side

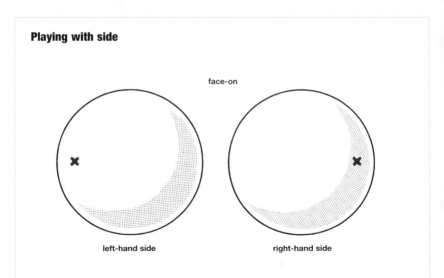

face-on

left-hand side   right-hand side

Players use side to change the angle at which the cue ball bounces off the cushion. If hit on the right, the cue ball will bounce to the right: this is known as 'side'. If hit on the left, it will bounce to the left: this is known as 'check side'.

BACKSPIN

When a cue ball is struck just a little below centre, it is given minimal backspin. The ball will spin in the opposite direction to that in which it is travelling, causing it to stop after it has struck the object ball. This is very useful, for example, in a straight shot, if the object ball is very close to the pocket and you want to stop the cue ball from following the object ball into it.

Close control – using side and backspin – is crucial when breakbuilding among a pack of reds. Here Ding Junhui shows the skills you need.

THE SCREW SHOT

The lower the cue ball is struck, the more backspin will be imparted to it. The screw shot is achieved by hitting the cue ball well below the centre, thus giving it a more powerful backspin. This causes the cue ball to go into reverse, or to 'screw back', after it has struck the object ball. The distance the cue ball will screw back after striking the object ball depends on how low you strike the cue ball, and how much spin, or screw, you impart to it.

Screw shot technique

The screw shot is very difficult to execute. It is essential to have a correctly shaped cue tip, coupled with a good cue action. When playing the screw shot, keep your body still and your head down, and use the same smooth, firm action that you would employ on any other shot. If you overdo the power in an attempt to screw the ball a long distance, you will almost certainly lift your head. This will cause the cue tip to rise, and the cue ball will only screw back a few inches.

Practising the screw shot

Practise striking the cue ball at 1mm variants up the ball and observe how this affects the screwing distance of the ball. Don't expect to screw the cue ball more than 2–3 ft (60–90cm). Screwing the cue ball long distances requires some experience, a good tip and a fast bed cloth.

Playing the screw shot

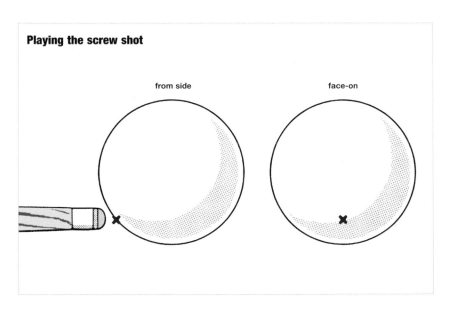

from side   face-on

Combinations

So far we've looked at what happens when we hit the cue ball above centre, below centre and to either side of centre. However, you can achieve more subtle effects by hitting other points on the cue ball. For example, you can apply topspin and side.

The best way to discover how these combinations affect the cue ball is to practise. Try a variety of cue-ball drills and learn what happens when the cue ball hits the object ball and cushions.

When applying side while attempting a pot, allow for the effect of the cue ball being pushed off line.

For breakbuilding around a pack of reds, you need to use all your shots – Stephen Hendry is the perfect role model.

THE SWERVE SHOT

In order to escape a snooker, sometimes it's necessary to make the cue ball swerve around an obstructing ball. The swerve shot can also let you pot a ball that you might otherwise have to leave for your opponent. It is achieved by striking the cue ball from above, either to the left or right, with the cue held in a more upright position (up to a maximum of about 45 degrees).

Technique

When playing a swerve shot, raise your bridge hand so that only the tips of your fingers are touching the table, allowing you to attack the cue ball from above. Using a not-too-powerful downward action, strike the cue ball at approximately one o'clock when using right-hand side and at eleven o'clock when using left-hand side. When you practise the shot, take note of the path the cue ball follows, and adjust the strength of the shot as necessary for different distances. Even for professionals, the swerve is not a particularly accurate shot in terms of positional play. But it is very useful in certain situations and is well worth practising.

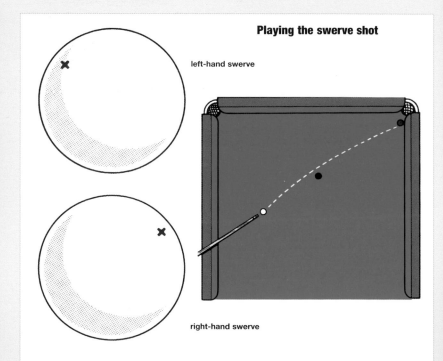

Playing the swerve shot

left-hand swerve

right-hand swerve

HOW DOES THE SWERVE SHOT WORK?

By striking downwards, most of the power that would have given the cue ball forward motion is absorbed by the table. This gives the spin more of a chance to affect the ball's movement, causing it to move sharply to the right or left. When the spin ceases, the ball returns towards its original line, completing the swerve.

THE STUN

The stun is a sharp, semi-powerful stroke that causes the cue ball to stop soon after contact with the object ball. The stun can be played with backspin to make the cue ball stop dead. Or it can be played to

the centre of the ball or with varying amounts of topspin (the stun run-through) to make the ball roll a certain distance forward after hitting the object ball. The stun shot is so versatile and gives the player such control over the cue ball that it is well worth practising.

The stun run-through

This is arguably the most useful type of stun shot, so it's worth discussing in a little more detail. First, place the cue ball and object ball 12–18 in (30–45cm) apart. Aim the cue tip to the dead centre of the cue ball (point **A** in the diagram) and punch firmly (do not roll the ball). After contact, the cue ball will travel forwards approximately 3 in (8cm). Now try varying the point where the tip strikes the cue ball. Move upwards from the centre in 1mm variants, as shown in the diagram. You will notice that the higher up the ball you strike, the further the cue ball will travel after hitting the object ball.

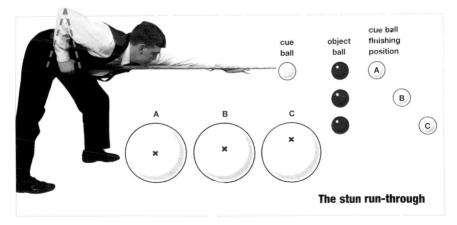

The stun run-through

POTTING

The art of potting is, of course, fundamental to snooker. Naturally it's important to have a good stance, excellent vision and a smooth cueing action, but it's also vital to hit the object ball in the right place in order to send it into a pocket. You have to know what will and what won't pot. Most crucial of all, you must maintain a smooth, steady cueing action regardless of the difficulty of the pot or the stage of the game you're at. The best way to gain potting confidence is to set up the cue ball and object ball for a particular shot and then practise it.

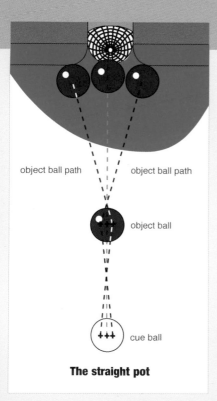

object ball path

object ball path

object ball

cue ball

The straight pot

The straight pot

In the case of the straight pot, the line of aim goes through the centre of the cue ball, the centre of the object ball and the centre of the pocket. It sounds simple in theory, and probably the only reason for missing the straight pot is incorrect sighting of the cue ball (see pages 28–9 for more information about sighting). As you can see in the diagram, if you strike the cue ball left of centre, it will squeeze to the right and the object ball will miss the pocket to the left; if the cue ball is struck right of centre, the opposite occurs. Place the cue ball 12–15 in (30–38cm) from the object ball and try applying varying degrees of side, observing the effects each time.

Back foot aligned with cue line. Many professionals adopt this stance when attempting a straight pot.

Back foot out to the right. Many uncoached players do this, and it often works.

The angled pot

Few pots are perfectly straight. It's therefore very important to learn how to judge angles so that you can find the right spot on the object ball in order to pot it. Judging potting angles is not something easily taught, and is really just a matter of practice. You can estimate the angles more easily by looking from the cue ball to the pocket at a low angle.

- If the object ball is fully covered by the cue ball, then it is a straight pot.

- If the cue ball covers three-quarters of the object ball, then it is a three-quarter-ball pot.

- If half the ball is covered, then it is a half-ball pot.

- If quarter of the ball is covered, then it is a quarter-ball cut.

THE FEET

The positioning of the foot can play a crucial part in the ability to hit a straight pot. Either through instinct or by a conscious decision, a number of professionals place the right back foot (if a right-handed player) straight down the cue line (see photograph above). It doesn't matter which position you choose, so long as it is effective for you.

> It is just as important to be accurate in your cueing and sighting when you play safe as when you are potting.

When attempting a fine cut from a distance of 3 ft (90cm) or more, the object ball should not be aimed at the centre of the pocket but at the lower edge if you are playing the shot with the nap – as the cue ball will drift with the nap, leading to a thick or thin object ball contact. If you are playing the shot against the nap, you will need to aim for the upper edge of the pocket.

Short- and long-range potting

With short-range potting, the balls have a short distance to travel and consequently have less opportunity to deviate from the intended path. However, even over short distances, a small amount of unintended side on the cue ball can be the difference between potting a ball and missing it. Naturally, any cueing errors are accentuated over longer distances, making longer pots far more difficult.

THE NAP

Your ability to pot over long distances is likely to be affected by the nap – the pile on the snooker tablecloth. It's therefore a good idea to take some time to study how the nap affects the movement of the balls on the playing surface. You can then make allowances for this when you come to play your shots.

The effects of the nap really become noticeable on long-range potting, especially when the ball is moving slowly. However, it can happen over short distances as well.

The nap runs from the baulk end to the black spot end. Its effects are different depending on whether you are playing against the nap (from the black spot end to the baulk end), playing with it, or playing across it (across the width of the table).

> No two snooker tables are exactly alike, and it is best to practise on a table before a game to observe the effects of the nap and the speed of the cloth.

Be sure to follow Steve
Davis and look closely
at the possible effects of the
nap on your shots.

The effects of the nap – cue-ball drift

When playing with the nap, as in Example 1, the cue ball will always try to straighten with the natural line of the nap. In other words, it will veer towards the spot end cushion rail. When playing against the nap, the cue ball will drift towards the side cushions.

Making allowances

Remember: the contact point on the object ball does not alter, but to hit that contact point requires you to make allowances for cue-ball drift. The longer the distance the cue ball must travel, the greater the allowance you must make.

On a long pot of about 6 ft (1.8m), such as the one shown in Example 1, even if the cue ball is travelling at a medium pace, it could drift by as much as 1–3 mm. At such a distance, even a small deviation like this could cause the pot to be missed by as much as 2–4 in (5–10cm).

Of course, one way of avoiding the effects of cue-ball drift is simply to strike the ball with a little more power, making it travel faster. To do this with the same accurate sighting and straight-line cue delivery takes practice.

Example 1 Here we see a pot of 6 ft (1.8m) playing from the baulk end (i.e. with the nap). The nap will pull the cue ball to the black spot end cushion (**A**). The broken line shows the path the cue ball must take to compensate for cue-ball drift. If the cue ball was directed down the unbroken line, it would make a thin contact to the right of centre on the object ball (**B**) and a consequent missed shot to the left. The arrow shows its continued path to the spot end top cushion.

Example 2 Here we see the effect of potting across the nap from the black spot end. The nap will pull the cue ball to the side cushion (**E**). If the object ball is nearer to the cue ball (**D**), it will be the object ball that drifts with the nap. In that event, a very small allowance for drift is required, aiming at a point above the top side of the pocket entry (**F**). Even an apparently simple, straight pot (**C**) to the centre pocket, played with some pace, will cause the object ball to drift with the nap to the left and the pot can be missed off the top of the pocket angle (**F**).

Example 1

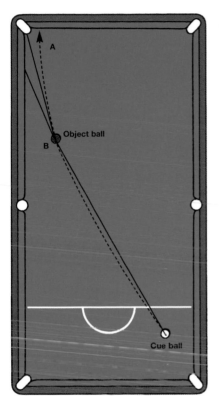

Baulk end cushion rail

> **Don't forget to allow for cue-ball drift during safety play.**

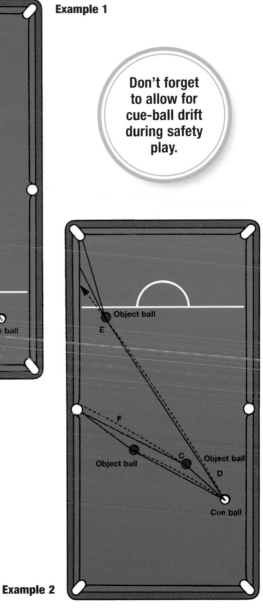

Example 2

Spot end cushion rail

HOW TO PRACTISE

With snooker, as with any sport, practice makes perfect. It will help you to consolidate the skills you are acquiring and give you more confidence when playing competitively.

CUE-BALL CONTROL

Being able to pot the ball is one thing, but if you want to be able to build a break you have to learn how to control the position of the cue ball AFTER it has struck the object ball. The practice shots described on the following pages will help you learn to do just that. As always, remember that stance and cueing discipline are of paramount importance.

▶ Cue-ball control is essential for your ability to build breaks.

Mid-table cue-ball control (1)

Place the blue ball on the centre spot, then place the cue ball at a slight angle to the blue ball, approximately 12–15 in (30–40cm) away (as illustrated). Set any three balls in a line across the table around the pink spot. These are the target balls. Strike the cue ball as shown on positions A, B and C. Play it as a punch shot. Note the different angles produced, and how close it ends up to the target balls. Obviously, when playing a game the target balls would be an imaginary target point.

Practising mid-table cue-ball control (1)

Mid-table cue-ball control (2)

Place the black ball on its spot. Set the cue ball on a predetermined chalk mark. Position any three balls (as illustrated). Strike the cue ball on positions A, B and C to pot the black and obtain positional contact on the three balls.

Practising mid-table cue-ball control (2)

Dislodging balls from the cushion

Practise this shot by placing the cue ball on a predetermined mark on the table and the black on the black spot. Place three balls along the side cushion. Try to pot the black by striking the cue ball on the positions marked **A**, **B** and **C**. Play it as a punch shot with medium power. See if you can dislodge the target balls. This is a useful exercise for learning the stun shot.

Try the stun off the cushion as shown on page 49 and observe the different effects. In all cases, do not let the object ball touch the cushion prior to entering the pocket.

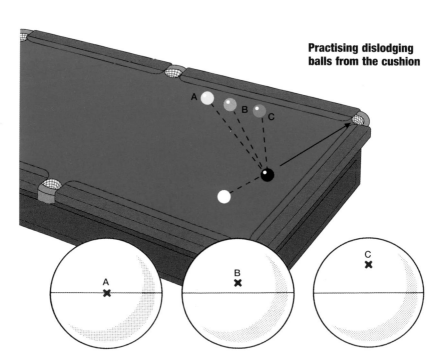

Practising dislodging balls from the cushion

The stun off the cushion

This is one of the most important shots to practise, because a player will frequently be confronted with an object ball near the top cushion. Place the cue ball in position X as shown in the diagram. Play it at the various points up the centre line of the cue ball, marked A, B, C and D, with the aim of potting the red. As you can see, this shot can send the cue ball to a range of finishing positions and thus help you achieve position on the black. Play it as a punch shot.

Remember, it is essential that the object ball is not allowed to come into contact with the cushion before entering the pocket opening – allow up to 10mm clearance. Practise playing the cue ball along a path parallel to the cushion using varying strengths and note the distance you can afford in order to clear the cushion and still get the pot.

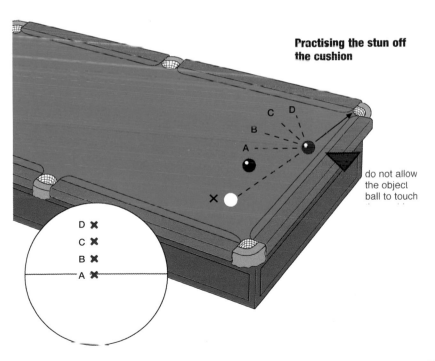

Practising the stun off the cushion

do not allow the object ball to touch

Running side

Side spin that widens the angle at which the cue ball bounces off the cushion is called running side. In situations where the potting line is narrow in relation to the pocket opening, you will need to play your shot with top and running side.

In Shot **A** in the illustration, the cue ball is closer than the object ball to the cushion. If you play the shot with running side, the cue ball will bounce off the side cushion to give you position on the black.

Don't forget to allow for the squeeze created by the right-hand side on the cue ball, which will send the object ball marginally further to the left than if you had hit the plain ball.

In other words, your target point should be slightly to the right of the pocket opening.

With Shot **B**, the cue ball is further than the object ball from the cushion. The line of follow-through is onto the top cushion, to the side cushion, and into position on the black.

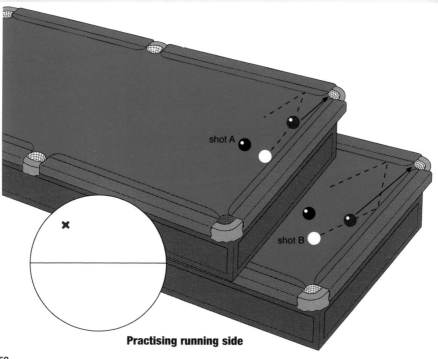

Practising running side

Check side

Side spin that narrows the angle at which the cue ball bounces off the cushion is called check side. This shot is very important when clearing the colours. Play it with left-hand side and top. Note the object ball 'target allowance' when assessing the shot. The cue ball is squeezed by the applied left-hand side which creates a thinner contact on the object ball, thus affecting the shot. It must be played firmly, otherwise the cue ball will swing back to the left and the shot could be missed. If the cue ball is struck with the right pace, it will first strike the right-hand cushion, return to the left-hand cushion, then travel to a point where good position on the brown ball can be attained.

Practising these moves until you are confident will pay dividends in a real game.

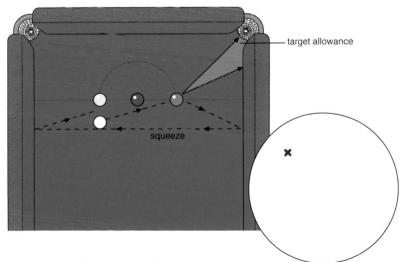

target allowance

squeeze

Practising check side

OTHER IMPORTANT SHOTS

The break

When breaking off, the target point should be the end red (**A** in the diagram). Use right-hand side on the cue ball. This will 'push' the cue ball over to make contact with the penultimate red, thus allowing the path of the cue ball as shown. It is very important to remember to allow for this 'push'.

Do not play the shot slowly because this will cause the cue ball to swerve to the right, resulting in thin contact of the end red or even a complete miss. Play the break as a firm punch with follow-through.

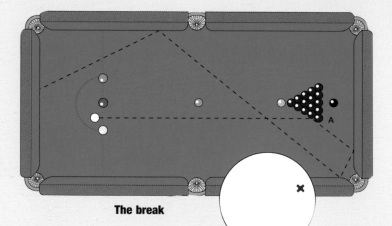

The break

> The break-off is a very important shot to master, as it can set the tone for a whole frame of snooker. It is therefore a good idea to break off in the same way every time.

Clearing the colours

The potting of the colours is a vital aspect of any match because the majority of games are decided by the number of points accumulated on the last six balls of the frame. Arguably the most crucial shot in a frame is the positional shot off the colour that follows the final red, before the actual colour sequence is commenced.

The diagrams on the right are not the only routes you can follow when clearing the colours, but they are easier than any alternatives.

Yellow – A full three-quarter-ball angle contact on the yellow allows the opportunity to play a firm stun shot (without the cue ball touching the cushion) onto the green.

Green – A three-quarter-ball angle on the green with a firm stun should leave a half-ball contact on the brown, without the cue ball touching the cushion.

Brown – A half-ball contact on the brown should allow a natural stun on the side cushion, leaving a three-quarter-ball contact on the blue.

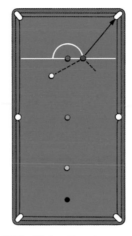
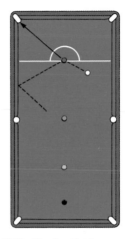

Blue – Play the three-quarter-ball contact as a plain ball run-through to leave a three quarter-ball contact on the pink.

Pink – Play the three-quarter ball contact as a firm stun to leave a comfortable position on the black.

Black – Pot the black and the frame is over (if the scores are level, the black would be re-spotted and the next shot taken from baulk).

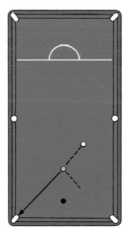

SNOOKER WORLD CHAMPIONS 1927–2005

The World Snooker Championship was first held in 1927, with the winner – Joe Davis – receiving £6 10 shillings prize money.

Typically an annual tournament, there have been a few exceptions down the years – in 1952 a disagreement between the then governing body (the Billiards Association and Control Council – BA&CC) and some of the players led to two tournaments; and between 1964-1968 it was held as a challenge tournament leading to irregular dates for matches.

Year	Champion	Opponent
1927	Joe Davis	Tom Dennis
1928	Joe Davis	Fred Lawrence
1929	Joe Davis	Tom Dennis
1930	Joe Davis	Tom Dennis
1931	Joe Davis	Tom Dennis
1932	Joe Davis	Clark McConachy
1933	Joe Davis	Willie Smith
1934	Joe Davis	Tom Newman
1935	Joe Davis	Willie Smith
1936	Joe Davis	Horace Lindrum
1937	Joe Davis	Horace Lindrum
1938	Joe Davis	Sidney Smith
1939	Joe Davis	Sidney Smith
1940	Joe Davis	Fred Davis
1941–1945	No tournament held	
1946	Joe Davis	Horace Lindrum
1947	Walter Donaldson	Fred Davis
1948	Fred Davis	Walter Donaldson
1949	Fred Davis	Walter Donaldson
1950	Walter Donaldson	Fred Davis
1951	Fred Davis	Walter Donaldson
1952 *	Horace Lindrum	Clark McConachy
1952 **	Fred Davis	Walter Donaldson
1953	Fred Davis	Walter Donaldson
1954	Fred Davis	Walter Donaldson
1955	Fred Davis	John Pulman
1956	Fred Davis	John Pulman
1957	John Pulman	John Rea
1958–1963	No tournament held	

* = BA&CC   ** = World Matchplay Championship

Year	Champion	Opponent
1964	John Pulman	Fred Davis
	John Pulman	Rex Williams
1965	John Pulman	Fred Davis
	John Pulman	Rex Williams
	John Pulman	Fred Van Rensburg
1966	John Pulman	Fred Davis
1967	No tournament held	
1968	John Pulman	Eddie Charlton
1969	John Spencer	Gary Owen
1970	Ray Reardon	John Pulman
1971	John Spencer	Warren Simpson
1972	Alex Higgins	John Spencer
1973	Ray Reardon	Eddie Charlton
1974	Ray Reardon	Graham Miles
1975	Ray Reardon	Eddie Charlton
1976	Ray Reardon	Alex Higgins
1977	John Spencer	Cliff Thorburn
1978	Ray Reardon	Perrie Mans
1979	Terry Griffiths	Dennis Taylor
1980	Cliff Thorburn	Alex Higgins
1981	Steve Davis	Doug Mountjoy
1982	Alex Higgins	Ray Reardon
1983	Steve Davis	Cliff Thorburn
1984	Steve Davis	Jimmy White
1985	Dennis Taylor	Steve Davis
1986	Joe Johnson	Steve Davis
1987	Steve Davis	Joe Johnson
1988	Steve Davis	Terry Griffiths
1989	Steve Davis	John Parrott
1990	Stephen Hendry	Jimmy White
1991	John Parrott	Jimmy White
1992	Stephen Hendry	Jimmy White
1993	Stephen Hendry	Jimmy White
1994	Stephen Hendry	Jimmy White
1995	Stephen Hendry	Nigel Bond
1996	Stephen Hendry	Peter Ebdon
1997	Ken Doherty	Stephen Hendry
1998	John Higgins	Ken Doherty
1999	Stephen Hendry	Mark Williams
2000	Mark Williams	Matthew Steven
2001	Ronnie O'Sullivan	John Higgins
2002	Peter Ebdon	Stephen Hendry
2003	Mark Williams	Ken Doherty
2004	Ronnie O'Sullivan	Graeme Dott
2005	Shaun Murphy	Matthew Stevens

MAXIMUM BREAKS

Making a maximum break is one of the highlights of a player's career. The highest possible break (where no fouls have been committed) is 147 – 15 reds, 15 blacks and all the colours. It is an incredible achievement.

It is possible to score up to 155 in a break – if your opponent fouls and leaves you with a free ball, effectively an extra red which must be followed by a colour. The highest recorded break is by Tony Drago, in 1998. He scored 149.

Here are some other key facts about maximum breaks:
- The first official maximum break was by Joe Davis in 1955.
- The first maximum in professional competition was by John Spencer in 1979 (against Cliff Thorburn).
- Steve Davis made the first televised 147 in 1982.
- Cliff Thorburn made the first maximum at the Snooker World Championships in 1983.
- The fastest recorded 147 is by Ronnie O'Sullivan – he took just 5 minutes and 20 seconds (in 1997).
- Stephen Hendry holds the record for the most maximum clearances in professional competition – he has achieved it 8 times (7 of these were televised, which is another record).

Below is a list of some of the more recent maximum clearances in professional competition.

Date	Player	Opponent	Event
November 1992	Peter Ebdon	Ken Doherty	UK Championship
September 1994	David McDonnell	Nic Barrow	British Open
27 April 1995	Stephen Hendry	Jimmy White	Embassy World Championship
25 November 1995	Stephen Hendry	Gary Wilkinson	UK Championship
5 January 1997	Stephen Hendry	Ronnie O'Sullivan	Liverpool Victoria Charity Challenge
21 April 1997	Ronnie O'Sullivan	Mick Price	Embassy World Championship
September 1997	James Wattana	Pang Wei Guo	Catch China International
16 May 1998	Stephen Hendry	Ken Doherty	Doc. Marten's Premier League
10 August 1998	Adrian Gunnell	Mario Wehrmann	Thailand Masters

Date	Player	Opponent	Event
13 August 1998	Mehmet Husnu	Eddie Barker	China International
13 January 1999	Jason Prince	Ian Brumby	British Open
29 January 1999	Ronnie O'Sullivan	James Wattana	Regal Welsh Open
4 February 1999	Stuart Bingham	Barry Hawkins	UK Tour Event
22 March 1999	Nick Dyson	Adrian Gunnell	UK Tour Event
6 April 1999	Graeme Dott	David Roe	British Open
19 September 1999	Stephen Hendry	Peter Ebdon	British Open
21 September 1999	Barry Pinches	Joe Johnson	Regal Welsh Open
13 October 1999	Ronnie O'Sullivan	Graeme Dott	Grand Prix
4 November 1999	Karl Burrows	Adrian Rosa	Benson & Hedges Championship
22 November 1999	Stephen Hendry	Paul Wykes	UK Championship
21 January 2000	John Higgins	Dennis Taylor	Nations Cup
24 March 2000	John Higgins	Jimmy White	Benson & Hedges Championship
24 March 2000	Stephen Maguire	Phaitoon Phonbun	Regal Scottish Open
5 April 2000	Ronnie O'Sullivan	Quinten Hann	Regal Scottish Open
25 October 2000	Marco Fu	Ken Doherty	Regal Scottish Masters
7 November 2000	David McLellan	Steve Meakin	Benson & Hedges Championship
19 November 2000	Nick Dyson	Rob Milkins	UK Championship
25 February 2001	Stephen Hendry	Mark Williams	Malta Grand Prix
17 October 2001	Ronnie O'Sullivan	Drew Henry	LG Cup
12 November 2001	Shaun Murphy	Adrian Rosa	Benson & Hedges Championship
28 October 2002	Tony Drago	Stuart Bingham	Benson & Hedges Championship
22 April 2003	Ronnie O'Sullivan	Marco Fu	Embassy World Championship
12 October 2003	John Higgins	Mark Williams	LG Cup
12 November 2003	John Higgins	Michael Judge	British Open
4 October 2004	John Higgins	Ricky Walden	Grand Prix
17 November 2004	David Gray	Mark Selby	UK Championship
20 April 2005	Mark Williams	Robert Milkins	Embassy World Championship
22 November 2005	Stuart Bingham	Marcus Campbell	The Masters Qualifiers

THE WORLD PROFESSIONAL BILLIARDS & SNOOKER ASSOCIATION

The World Professional Billiards & Snooker Association (WPBSA) is the governing body for professional billiards and snooker around the world.

Formed in 1968 as the Professional Billiards Players' Association with only eight members, the WPBSA is responsible for all policy making which is made by a Board of Directors who are elected by the members. It deals specifically with the rules and regulations of the sport and is also responsible for world rankings.

The WPBSA also acts in a disciplinary capacity and was one of the first professional sporting bodies to introduce a comprehensive drug testing policy under International Olympic Committee (IOC) guidelines.

You can contact the WSPBSA at:

Ground Floor
Albert House
111–117 Victoria Street
Bristol BS1 6AX

World Snooker

World Snooker is the commercial arm of the WPBSA. It is responsible for running and administrating snooker's professional circuit, including prestigious ranking tournaments such as the World Championship, UK Championship and the Grand Prix, as well as invitation events such as the Masters. As the owner of the sport's commercial rights, World Snooker also negotiates sponsorship for tournaments as well as television contracts.

You can contact World Snooker at:

14–16 Great Portland St
London W1W 8QW

You can also visit the website at:

www.worldsnooker.com.

The website contains lots of useful information and links.

GLOSSARY

All games pockets Pocket nets connected to runners allowing the balls to be retrieved without inserting the hand from the top (also known as 'empire rails').

Backspin The effect of striking the cue ball below centre.

Bed The playing surface, consisting of five equal pieces of machined slate 1–3 in (3–8cm) thick.

Bed cloth The cloth covering the playing surface.

Break A sequence of scoring shots.

Break-off The opening shot of a frame in which the striker must play at the triangle of reds.

Check side Side spin that narrows the angle at which the cue ball rebounds from the cushion.

Clearance A sequence of scoring shots that continues until the player has potted all the balls left on the table.

Cushion cloth The cloth that covers the rubbers.

Cushion rail The exterior wooden surface of the table, in six parts, drilled to take the pocket plates.

Cushion rubbers The rubber strips that are glued onto the inside face of the cushion rails.

D The semi-circle inscribed on the baulk line from which all strokes must be played when the striker is in hand, for example when breaking off.

Double A shot in which the object ball is potted after striking one or more cushions.

Double kiss A second contact on the object ball.

Drag shot A long shot that is played with normal strength and plenty of backspin, the effect being to slow down the cue ball late in its journey.

Fluke A shot that results in a fortuitous bonus, such as an unintentional pot or snooker.

Forcing shot A stroke played considerably above medium pace.

Foul stroke A shot or action that infringes one of the rules of the game, thereby incurring a specified penalty.

Frame of the table All the woodwork that makes up the table base.

Free ball The result of a snooker caused by a foul stroke. The player snookered in this way (i.e. he cannot hit both extremities of the object ball) may nominate any coloured ball as a red for the purposes of his next shot. If he pots it he scores one, and then nominates a colour in the usual manner. If there are no reds left on the table, he nominates one of the colours as a free ball, and if he pots it he scores the value of the lowest value ball on the table. The nominated colour is re-spotted and he then plays the colours in sequence.

Full-ball contact Striking the object ball full face, so that all of it is covered by the cue ball at the moment of impact.

Half-ball contact Striking the object ball so that half of it is covered by the cue ball at the moment of impact.

Half-butt A matching 7.5 ft (2.3m) cue and rest required to reach the cue ball for any shots too distant to reach with the normal rest.

In-off A shot resulting in the cue ball being pocketed – a foul stroke.

Kick An unclean contact between cue ball and object ball caused by chalk, dust or anything that results in the de-glossing of a portion of one of the balls. It distorts the angle of deflection and sometimes causes the cue ball to lift off slightly.

Kiss Contact by the cue ball on a second (or subsequent) object ball.

Massé A shot in which the cue strikes almost vertically down on one side of the cue ball, imparting maximum swerve. It is much more common in billiards than snooker.

Maximum break A scoring sequence in which the player pots all 15 reds, 15 blacks and all the colours to score a maximum total of 147.

Nap The grain of the cloth that is fixed to the bed. The nap runs from the baulk end to the spot end.

Natural angle The angle the cue ball will take after striking the object ball at medium pace without spin of any sort.

Plain-ball striking Striking the centre of the cue ball, i.e. no topspin, backspin or side.

Plant A position in which one object ball is played onto another object ball in order to pot the latter.

Pocket leathers The leather that is stitched and shaped onto the pocket plates at the impact point of the ball.

Pocket nets Nets that act as the holding receptacles for the balls.

Pocket opening The point where the ball enters the pocket.

Pocket plates The pocket supports to which the leather and pocket nets are affixed. Much older tables have surface brass fittings fixed to the top of the cushion rails, and quite often the cushion rail is quite narrow. Modern tables usually have invisible pocket plates, concealed with a metal peg in the ends of the cushion rails.

Pocket weight A slow shot with just sufficient pace to carry the object ball to the pocket.

Power shot A forcing shot of great pace.

Quarter-ball contact Striking the ball so that a quarter of it is covered by the cue ball at the moment of impact.

Rest The smallest and least cumbersome of the implements used to reach the cue ball when it is beyond comfortable range for a conventional bridge.

Running side Side spin that widens the angle at which the cue ball rebounds from the cushion.

Safe position A lie from which a scoring strike is unlikely.

Safety shot A defensive stroke that aims not to score but to leave the opponent in a safe position.

Screw To impart heavy backspin to the cue ball, the result being a stun, screw or drag shot, depending on factors of distance and pace.

Screw shot A shot in which the cue ball recoils from the object ball on contact (if full ball), or leaves it at wider than the natural angle if the contact is angled.

Set A type of plant in which the two object balls are touching.

Shot to nothing A tactical shot in which a player attempts to pot the red ball and leave the cue ball in the baulk area of the table. If he misses the pot, the cue ball will be safe. If he pots the ball, the cue ball may finish in a good position to pot one of the three baulk colours.

Side spin Usually referred to as 'side', this is the effect of striking the cue ball to the right or left of centre. It will either widen or narrow the angle at which the cue ball rebounds from a cushion, and can be used in conjunction with either backspin or topspin.

Snooker A lie from which the player is prevented from hitting both sides of the object ball by an intervening ball that is not on.

Spider A rest with a raised head, allowing bridging at a distance over an intervening ball or balls. There are variations on the spider, devised for particularly awkward positions.

Spots The points on the cloth on which the various colours sit.

Stun shot A shot in which the cue ball stops dead on contact with the object ball (if full ball), or leaves it at a wider than normal angle (but not as wide as a screw shot) if the contact is angled. Stun shots usually require the application of screw, but where the cue ball and object ball are very close together, stun may be achieved by central striking or even slightly higher.

Stun run-through shot A shot at close quarters where the object is to retard the cue ball's forward momentum after contact with the object ball, but not kill it totally.

Swerve The exaggerated side spin achieved by striking down on one side of the cue ball, the object being to curve the cue ball around an obstructing ball.

Three-quarter-ball contact Striking the object ball so that three-quarters of it is covered by the cue ball at the moment of impact.

Three-quarter butt A 9 ft (2.75m) version of the half-butt, needed only rarely.

Topspin The effect achieved by striking the cue ball above centre.

INDEX

angles 32, 35, 41, 47, 50, 51
arm 22, 24, 25, 26, 27, 31

backspin 35, 36, 39
baize 6, 8
ball on 19, 20, 21
balls (see also cue ball, object balls) 6, 9, 16
  bridging 31
  colours (see also red, yellow, green, brown, blue, pink, black balls) 52
  forfeit 19, 20
  nap 42
  potting 17
  rules 18, 19
  screw shot 36
  side 34
  stance 27
  topspin 33
baulk 6, 8, 42, 44, 45, 53
baulk line 7, 33
BBC 5
black ball 16, 17, 53
  cushion 49
  fouls 20, 21
  rules 19
  running side 50
black spot 6, 7, 8, 48
black spot end 42, 44
blue ball 16, 53
  forfeit 20
  fouls 20
blue spot 7
break 17, 46
break-off 52
breakbuilding 35, 37
bridge 11, 14, 24, 25, 38
bridging 30–31, 33
brown ball 16, 51, 53
brown spot 7
butt 10

cannons 20
centre spot 7, 47
chalk 9, 12, 13, 15

check side 35, 51
close control 35
cloth 6, 9, 36, 42
colours 16, 17
  check side 51
  clearing 52
  rules 18
  snookering 21
combination shots 37
cue 6, 10–13, 19
  fouls 20
  rest 31
  rules 18
  sighting 28, 29
  stance 23, 24, 25, 26, 27
  swerve shot 38
  topspin 33
cue action 22, 32, 36
cue arm 22, 27
cue ball 9, 10, 16, 18
  backspin 35
  break 52
  bridging 30
  check side 51
  combination shots 37
  control 4, 34, 46–47
  drift 44, 45
  fouls 20, 21
  in hand 7
  kicks 12
  nap effects 44
  plain ball 32
  potting 40, 41, 42
  rest 14, 31
  rules 18, 19
  screw shot 36
  shots 32
  side 34, 35
  sighting 29, 31, 33
  snookering 21
  stance 23, 26, 27
  stun 39
  swerve shot 38, 39
  topspin 33
cue ferrule leveller 12
cue line 41
cue tip 10, 11–13, 15

rules 18
screw shot 36
shapers 15
stance 27
stun 39
cueing 26, 30, 40, 42, 46
cushion 6, 7, 9, 53
   angle 32, 35, 50
   bridging 30, 31
   care of the table 8
   check side 51
   combination shots 37
   cue ball drift 44

D 7
Davis, Joe 4, 5, 31
Davis, Steve 5, 43

Embassy World Championship 5

feet 18, 41
   stance 22, 23, 24, 25, 27
ferrule 10, 12, 15
first impact 20, 21
follow-through 23, 24, 50, 52
forfeit 19, 20
fouls 18–21
frames 5, 17, 52, 53

green ball 16, 19, 20, 21, 53
green spot 7

half-ball 41, 53
half-butt rest 14
hand,
   bridging 30, 31
   stance 24, 25, 27
Hendry, Stephen 20, 35, 37
Higgins, John 31
hook rest 14

in hand 7
in-off 18

jump shot 18

kicks 12

left-eyed sighting style 28, 29
left-handed players 22
legs, stance 22, 23
lining up 24, 27, 29
long cue 14
long rest 14

match 17
miscues 13
Murphy, Shaun 5

nap 6, 8, 42, 43, 44
nominated ball 19, 20, 21

O'Sullivan, Ronnie 19
object ball 16, 32, 36
   backspin 35
   combination shots 37
   cue ball drift 44
   cushion 49
   plain ball 32
   potting 40, 41, 42
   side 34, 50, 51
   stance 27
   stun 39
   topspin 33

pack 35, 37
penalties 19, 20, 21
pink ball 8, 16, 19, 20, 53
pink spot 7, 47
plain ball 32, 33, 50, 53
pocket 6, 7
   backspin 35
   cue ball drift 44
   fouls 20, 21
   potting 17, 40, 41, 42
   rules 18
   running side 50
   stance 23
points 16, 17, 19, 20, 21, 52
position 22, 23, 24, 27, 32, 41
   bridging 31
potting 16, 17, 40–45
   colours 52
   cue ball drift 44
   cushion 49

fouls 20, 21
rules 18
running side 50
side 37
stance 22
swerve shot 38
punch shot 47, 48, 49, 52
push 32
pyramid spot 7

quarter-ball cut 41, 42

rack 15
red balls 16, 17
  break 35, 37, 52
  colours 52
  cushion 49
  forfeit 19, 20
  fouls 21
  rules 18, 19
  snookering 21
  triangle 15
referee 8, 20, 21
rest 6, 14, 18, 31
right-eyed sighting style 29
right-hand side 52
rules 18, 20
running side 50

screw shot 31, 36
side 10, 34, 35
  break 52
  check 51
  combination shots 37
  potting 40, 42
  rest 31
  shots 32
  sighting 29
  topspin 33
side cushion 44, 48
sighting 28–29, 31, 33, 40, 44
snooker 19, 20, 21, 38
spider rest 14
spin 32, 36, 39, 50
spot end 44, 45
spots 7, 9, 16, 17, 18, 47
stance 22–27, 40, 46

standard rest 14
Stevens, Matthew 5
straight pot 23, 32, 40, 41, 44
straight-line cue delivery 44
stun shot 25, 39, 48, 49, 53
swan rest 14
swerve shot 38, 39

table 5, 6–9, 42
  the game 16, 17, 18
Taylor, Dennis 5
television 5
three-quarter-ball 41, 53
top side 50, 51
topspin (top) 33, 37, 39
triangle 15, 16
two-eyed sighting style 28

Williams, Mark 17
world championship 5
World Professional Billiards & Snooker
  Association (WPBSA) 19, 58

yellow ball 16, 19, 20, 53
yellow spot 7